Editor-in-Chief and Founder:
  Lyndon H. LaRouche, Jr.
Editorial Board: *Lyndon H. LaRouche, Jr. , Helga Zepp-LaRouche, Robert Ingraham, Tony Papert, Gerald Rose, Dennis Small, Jeffrey Steinberg, William Wertz*
Co-Editors: *Robert Ingraham, Tony Papert*
Managing Editor: *Nancy Spannaus*
Technology: *Marsha Freeman*
Books: *Katherine Notley*
Ebooks: *Richard Burden*
Graphics: *Alan Yue*
Photos: *Stuart Lewis*
Circulation Manager: *Stanley Ezrol*

INTELLIGENCE DIRECTORS
Counterintelligence: *Jeffrey Steinberg, Michele Steinberg*
Economics: *John Hoefle, Marcia Merry Baker, Paul Gallagher*
History: *Anton Chaitkin*
Ibero-America: *Dennis Small*
Russia and Eastern Europe: *Rachel Douglas*
United States: *Debra Freeman*

INTERNATIONAL BUREAUS
Bogotá: *Miriam Redondo*
Berlin: *Rainer Apel*
Copenhagen: *Tom Gillesberg*
Houston: *Harley Schlanger*
Lima: *Sara Madueño*
Melbourne: *Robert Barwick*
Mexico City: *Gerardo Castilleja Chávez*
New Delhi: *Ramtanu Maitra*
Paris: *Christine Bierre*
Stockholm: *Ulf Sandmark*
United Nations, N.Y.C.: *Leni Rubinstein*
Washington, D.C.: *William Jones*
Wiesbaden: *Göran Haglund*

ON THE WEB
e-mail: eirns@larouchepub.com
www.larouchepub.com
www.executiveintelligencereview.com
www.larouchepub.com/eiw
Webmaster: *John Sigerson*
Assistant Webmaster: *George Hollis*
Editor, Arabic-language edition: *Hussein Askary*

EIR (ISSN 0273-6314) *is published weekly (50 issues), by EIR News Service, Inc., P.O. Box 17390, Washington, D.C. 20041-0390. (703) 777-9451*

European Headquarters: E.I.R. GmbH, Postfach Bahnstrasse 9a, D-65205, Wiesbaden, Germany
Tel: 49-611-73650
Homepage: http://www.eirna.com
e-mail: eirna@eirna.com
Director: Georg Neudecker

Montreal, Canada: 514-461-1557

Denmark: EIR - Danmark, Sankt Knuds Vej 11, basement left, DK-1903 Frederiksberg, Denmark. Tel.: +45 35 43 60 40, Fax: +45 35 43 87 57. e-mail: eirdk@hotmail.com.

Mexico City: EIR, Sor Juana Inés de la Cruz 242-2 Col. Agricultura C.P. 11360 Delegación M. Hidalgo, México D.F. Tel. (5525) 5318-2301 eirmexico@gmail.com

Canada Post Publication Sales Agreement #40683579

Postmaster: Send all address changes to *EIR*, P.O. Box 17390, Washington, D.C. 20041-0390.

Signed articles in *EIR* represent the views of the authors, and not necessarily those of the Editorial Board.

Great Minds Create Mankind's Future

EDITORIAL

Their Day Has Come, —And Gone!

July 21—That is the meaning of the two releases this month, the one of Britain's long-delayed Chilcot report into Tony Blair's criminal responsibility for the illegal Iraq war, and the other of the long-suppressed 28 pages of the report of the Joint Congressional Inquiry into 9/11, documenting the Saudi hand behind that butchery. It means that time is up at last for those blood-drooling dinosaurs Tony Blair, George W. Bush, Dick Cheney, and Barack Obama, after fifteen years of wars based on lies. They have destroyed the Middle East, drowned Europe in desperate refugees, and caused blood to be spilled on the streets across Europe and the United States,— all based on lies.

And don't believe that Tony Blair was merely the "poodle" of the non-functional George W. Bush. In fact, he instigated Bush on behalf of the British Queen who was really giving the orders. For example, the documentation Chilcot released included a note from Blair to Bush on Sept. 12, 2001, urging him to act immediately on "weapons of mass destruction." Although he did not yet single out Iraq in particular, Blair wrote, "Some of this will require action that some will balk at. But we are better to act *now* and explain and justify our actions than let the day be put off until some further, perhaps even worse catastrophe occurs. And I believe this is a real possibility." [emphasis in original]

And the Kingdom of Saudi Arabia had not run 9/11 on their own; they did so as an adjunct of the British

Empire, which is what the Saudi Kingdom has been ever since the British created it less than a century ago. The immediate roots of 9/11 go back to the long-running British-Saudi "Al-Yamamah" arms deal, which created a multibillion-dollar slush fund administered, in part, by 9/11 kingpin Prince Bandar bin Sultan, then Saudi Ambassador to Washington. (And it was Prime Minister Tony Blair who in 2006 personally ordered Britain's Attorney General to close down the investigation of Al-Yamamah.)

Their fifteen years of wars based on lies, their fifteen years of terrorism, have been a Dark Age of civilization. It is time to discard all of this; it is time to institute a human direction of human affairs, even if there are only a few people who actually know what it is to be human, and actually conceive themselves as human beings rather than as smart talking animals. At this moment, at the time of the threatened breakout of an uncontrollable financial collapse, perhaps beginning with Germany's Deutsche Bank, Lyndon LaRouche has put forward an emergency initiative to forestall that collapse by fostering the productivity of labor, which is human creative discovery, or true humanity. He has proposed an emergency rescue of Deutsche Bank, on condition that it immediately and drastically alter its policy, returning to that of its former Chairman Alfred Herrhausen, who was murdered by still-unidentified killers on Nov. 30, 1989.

At that moment, Herrhausen was one of those,

like Lyndon LaRouche and his wife, Helga Zepp-LaRouche, who were moving to ensure that the then ongoing fall of the Communist system, led to high-technology, high-productivity joint development of the countries which had been on both sides of the so-called "Iron Curtain." In October, 1988, Lyndon LaRouche already knew that the Berlin Wall would fall, and Germany could be reunified, before virtually anyone else did. At that time, he spoke publicly in Berlin to urge that Germany assist in the agro-industrial development of Poland, to launch such a unified East-West process of development. Within three months, LaRouche was framed and thrown in prison by George H.W. Bush. One year later, Herrhausen, in his turn, was assassinated five days before he was scheduled to give a speech to precisely the same effect, calling for the establishment of a development bank for Poland, modelled on Germany's postwar reconstruction bank, itself modelled on Franklin Roosevelt's Reconstruction Finance Corporation.

This whole subject is far deeper than can be indicated here, and its implications far broader. But the dinosaurs have had their day. Make way for the human beings.

EIR Contents

www.larouchepub.com Volume 43, Number 31, July 29, 2016

Schiller Institute

Cover This Week

On Easter Sunday, March 27, 2016, the Schiller Institute Chorus, partnering with the Foundation for the Revival of Classical Culture, performed Parts II and III of the Messiah, at the Visitation of the Blessed Virgin Mary Roman Catholic Church, Brooklyn, New York.

INTERVIEW WITH DIANE SARE

Mission to Manhattan

Diane Sare is a member of the LaRouche PAC Policy Committee and the managing director of the Schiller Institute New York City Chorus. EIR interviewed her on July 24 on the ongoing choral work which the Schiller Institute is carrying out in New York City, leading into a series of concerts planned for the period around September 11 of this year, the fifteenth anniversary of the 9/11 attacks.

EIR: The Schiller Institute will be participating in a series of concerts this September, concerts which are sponsored by the Foundation for the Revival of Classical Culture. These will be concerts of Mozart's *Requiem*, which will be held at four locations in the New York metropolitan area to commemorate the fifteenth anniversary of the attacks on 9/11. Diane, you have called this a *Living Memorial* to the victims of 9/11. What would you like to say, by way of introduction,

about the idea behind this initiative and how it came about?

Diane Sare: It first came about—there had been something under discussion as we came toward this fifteenth anniversary obviously—but a few months ago, one of our activists from Connecticut asked Mr. LaRouche about all those people who died on September 11 who have not,— that there has been no justice, because the truth of what occurred on that day has not fully come out (although I must say we are getting closer). Mr. LaRouche said that what we need is stronger than just a memorial, but a living memorial, that Americans have to face the humility of not having acted to secure justice after we had 3,000 people murdered on that day, September 11, 2001. I would just add that the recent release of the Chilcot Inquiry gets at some of this, but I have to say that because the truth was not told, what you have had since that date is a perpetuation of

EIRNS/Bob Wesser

Diane Sare conducting a performance of the Schiller Institute's Manhattan chorus Feb. 14, 2015.

murder, of injustice and murder.

We didn't go after Saudi Arabia; instead we invaded Iraq,— although I'm not proposing that war in any form would particularly be the solution to this. We overthrew Qaddafi in Libya. We have created a situation where we have 60 million refugees, and over 4,000 American soldiers have died in Iraq, Afghanistan, and these wars, not to mention that we have a staggering rate of soldier suicides. So part of the conception of the living memorial, at least in my mind, is that it is not being done so people can listen to some beautiful music that they associate with someone dying and feel bad about it, but that by that time we should actually determine that we will have secured justice, which means not only the release of the 28 pages that we have just seen, but that we dramatically change the policy direction of the government of the United States, away from the British and Saudi Empires, and take a giant step toward creating a world where such things as what occurred on September 11, 2001, do not happen again.

EIRNS/Margaret Greenspan

Diane Sare conducting a rehearsal of the Schiller Institute's Manhattan chorus, Sept. 9, 2015.

How It Started

EIR: I know it has been a long process leading up to this, and that the Schiller Institute now has three functioning choruses in New York City, one in Manhattan, one in Brooklyn, and one in Queens. Could you tell us a bit about the history of how these choruses came into existence and how they have developed over the recent months?

Sare: Sure. The Manhattan chorus is the senior chorus; I'll put it that way. That was created in,— it really came together in December 2014, shortly after Mr. LaRouche launched the Manhattan Project, and that began really in response to a situation which continues, unfortunately to this day. People may remember the case of Eric Garner, an African American man who was killed in a choke-hold, strangled in a choke-hold by a police officer, and the grand jury on Staten Island determined that there was no wrongdoing, there was no indictable offense—which, coming on the heels of what had happened in Ferguson, Missouri, caused a great deal of anger and rage.

It's clear that you have certain elements who would like to see, particularly, Manhattan ripped apart, with various antagonistic groups feeling threatened by and threatening each other. Dennis Speed and I had a discussion around Christmas—I have always wanted to perform Handel's *Messiah* for any purpose—and we said, why don't we perform the *Messiah* in Manhattan, dedicated to the principle that all human life is sacred. If we are going to do something that is befitting for human beings, it has to come from a noble standpoint.

So we did that sing-along performance, and on very short notice; about a hundred people showed up to sing, and out of that we created a community chorus which has grown steadily over that last year and a half to be a very solid group, with ebbs and flows, I would say, but probably when you pull it together for a performance, you have sixty people or so. We did a *Messiah* around Christmas the following year. One of the performances was in Brooklyn, so it seemed a natural process to start another chorus in Brooklyn; there were many people who wanted to be part of this. So that chorus is coming along.

We have some collaborators, Chinese Americans in Flushing, Queens, who have wanted to collaborate with us on the question of classical music. They, interestingly, are very interested in learning African American spirituals and western classical music, so we now have a chorus in Flushing, Queens. Like the Manhattan one, the choruses tend to start off very slowly. I think the most important factor is that the choir director has to be absolutely consistent—whether three people show up or thirty people show up, whether they know how to read music and sing in tune, or they don't know how to read music and don't sing in tune—and at a certain point the group has to see itself as a group, and becomes a real institution, which is where we are in Manhattan. We are getting close to that in Brooklyn, and I think the Queens one is going to take off soon. I wouldn't be surprised if, after the series of *Requiem* concerts, we might not also have a chorus that gets started in the Bronx.

EIR: All you need then is Staten Island! I know the choral work we've done in New York has also gone hand in hand with, and been a critical component of what Lyndon LaRouche initiated as the Manhattan Project. Now if you look at the totality of our work, the work of the Schiller Institute and the LaRouche movement in Manhattan and the greater New York City area, some people have described this as a *new paradigm* in organizing—one in which classical music, politics, and economics come together, where these are not separate things but a unified approach, and where music plays a critical role in the actual organizing. So in terms of this new paradigm, do you think that's true? And if so, what are your thoughts on that, and what are the deeper implications of that for the organizing process?

Sare: I do think it is true, and I will just stick for now to the choral aspect of this because it is multi-faceted. In terms of a paradigm, it would mean everything. On the question of the choral work *per se,* the Schiller Institute has a long history of musical work which is now coming together—from the *Manual on Tuning and Registration,* which John Sigerson, who is directing the chorus now, was involved in, which was a scientific proof of the necessity of the Verdi tuning, and the question of *bel canto*, to the kind of collaborators that we had over the years, such as Carlo Bergonzi on the tuning in particular and the Italian bel canto method, William Warfield, Sylvia Olden Lee, and Maestro [José] Briano who was there early on, who just passed away. We had some truly inspired collaborators, with the result that between John's dedication to the question of *bel canto* and proper placement, and the political organizing process that I've been involved in, what has occurred is that our chorus, although it is very young, or new relative to other choruses in the city, is quickly developing a reputation for itself because of the quality of the sound, and the quality of the warmth of the sound and the musicality.

The members of this chorus are aware that they have a particular mission in terms of the question of uplifting mankind, uplifting the culture of Manhattan and the United States, and it comes across in the singing. So, when we had done the *Messiah* last Easter—I guess it was the Easter performance—a singer who works with us who happens to rent out rehearsal spaces and has her own newsletter, sent out a link to the video of just one of the choruses, to all of the singers who rehearse in her rehearsal spaces, and she got some pretty amazing feedback which she forwarded on to me. "This chorus has an exceptional sound," "you can hear the counterpoint," "I can't believe all the words are intelligible," comments like that, which I have to say are highly unusual, particularly for an amateur chorus. Ours is an amateur chorus, not a paid professional chorus; in fact, people contribute to paying for the rehearsal space, so they are actually paying to be in this chorus, and I think ultimately it will be setting a new standard for what goes on in this city in terms of choral music.

Almost a Sacred Quality

EIR: In a conversation you and I had the other day, one of the ways you characterized how our chorus works was that, for many of the participants—and I may not be putting this in your words, so correct me if I'm wrong—for many of the participants, the chorus rehearsals have taken on almost the character of a haven, a place where people are able to relate to each other on a more profound level, and you also stated that many of the people who have become involved in our chorus have expressed deep appreciation for the opportunity to participate. Is there anything you would like to say about that?

Sare: Yes, and I think that this also gets at the questions of what the problems are and the difficulties are in keeping a chorus together, because we are in a society which is disintegrating, and the so-called average American life—whatever that means—is filled with economic hardship and chaos. I can give one example of many. We had a wonderful alto singer who had actually sung in an opera company in her native country before she came to the United States, and she was working in the United States for a family as an *au pair,* taking care of children, cooking, cleaning, and so on. That is very grueling, hard work, and she would come into the rehearsal every night,— at this point we were working on Bach's *Jesu Meine Freude,* and she would get there late, just having rushed over from this very difficult job, and the family would often come home late, and she would be late, and she would sit down and say, "I'm so happy to be here. I'm so happy to be singing Bach after this day I've been through."

I definitely have the sense that for many people in the chorus, the ability to do beautiful music,— there is almost a sacred quality to it, where they can get away from all the conflicts and the hardships of their day-to-

LaRouche PAC Policy Committee member Diane Sare organizing at Columbus Circle, Manhattan, July 21, 2016, for a new paradigm in which classical music, politics, and economics come together.

day lives, and come and participate in something which is really beautiful and uplifting and nourishing to the soul. And I would say that is also the difficulty, because you may have guessed from my earlier comments, if I were to count up all of the people who have been at *one* rehearsal it would be well over a hundred, maybe a couple of hundred people by now.

It takes a lot to recruit the people who stay. Even with people who stay for several months, things come up, they change jobs, there is a conflict at work, or they can't afford the subway fare to get to the rehearsal. There is just so much disruption in people's lives that the most difficult thing is to get a core group and have the same people show up, week-in and week-out, and that is obviously something that tends to slow down the progress of the chorus. It's a bigger factor now in the smaller, newer ones in Brooklyn and Flushing, because you might have the same number of people every week, but if they are different people, you don't make the progress you would like to. So at least Manhattan is a bit more stabilized, but we do still have that challenge of the migrant choral singers, I'll call it. I don't think it's from their lack of interest. To do this requires a lot of work and concentration, and people are leading really difficult and hectic lives, so it is hard for them to be consistent.

EIR: I think that covers it fairly well. Is there anything more you would like to say in summing up, in particular in regard to the upcoming performances of the *Requiem* and the work going into that, or any other final comments you would like to make?

Sare: Yes, there are a few things I'd like to add.

One of the performances in Brooklyn is going to be at a church which is part of a district where the entire fire brigade, I think it was forty-two men, rushed to their deaths on September 11. From Brooklyn it is a short trip to lower Manhattan; they rushed over there and were inside one of the towers when it collapsed. Every year this church has a service, a special mass, on September 11.

This year, since it is the fifteenth anniversary, and it also happens to fall on a Sunday, the Monsignor expressed an interest in performing the Mozart *Requiem* as part of this particular mass. And I think that is going to be an extremely moving and powerful performance. The other performances will be in the Bronx, there will be one in a major church in midtown Manhattan, and there will be one in Morristown, New Jersey, in which we will be collaborating with family members of the 9/11 victims. So each one of these will have a specific dimension to it, relating to what happened and where our country needs to go.

I would like to close by saying that, in my mind, I am thinking of a certain parallel—but perhaps it will be even more significant if we can bring about a victory in this case—to what Putin did in Palmyra, where the city was in ruins; it had been taken over by ISIS, a city that was 2,000 years old with that beautiful amphitheater which ISIS had desecrated by executing people on the stage. When Russia had worked with the Syrian government forces to liberate this city from ISIS, they held a concert, beginning with an incredible Bach *Chaconne* on that very stage in that amphitheater, by the Mariinsky Theater Orchestra conducted by Putin's friend, Valery Gergiev.

I think the reason why this was so powerful, is that it is an example of what is meant by victory. That is, the point is not just to crush ISIS because it is evil, but the point is to actually engage mankind in doing the good, and to demonstrate that the principle of human civilization is a principle of beauty of the human race as a beautiful creative species. That really is the idea of the 9/11 concerts, and I think it is very urgent right now to remind Americans of it. As Americans are reminded of this, I think that their necessary courage in defeating what has led our nation into this mess will be greater.

EIR: Very good. Thank you.

Helga Zepp-LaRouche Renews Call For Banning Violent Videos

July 24 —Speaking to the U.S. La-Rouche movement today, Helga Zepp-LaRouche addressed the terrorist killing of nine people in Munich by a lone shooter.

Zepp-LaRouche said, "The new surprise is that the killer was *not* an Islamic extremist; the shooter was a devotee of violent video games," and was imitating previous mass shooters also conditioned by long use of those first-person shooter games and videos.

Zepp-LaRouche said two actions must be taken worldwide:

1. Citing German Interior Minister Thomas de Mazière's connection of the Munich mass killings to violent videos, she said that an international ban on violent video games, including banning them from the Internet, must be carried out.
2. International cooperation with Russia against terrorism, as President Vladimir Putin proposed to the UN General Assembly in September 2015.

The Munich teenage shooter, Ali David Sonboly, lured young people to McDonald's on the fifth anniversary of the mass killing of 77 youths by Anders Breivik

PRNewsFoto

The systemic degeneration of the world's youth. Here, a team member during the World Cyber Games CounterStrike final.

in Norway in 2011. The Munich shooter also had material on a mass shooting at a school in Bavaria in 2009. Sonboly offered to buy free food at McDonald's for anyone who came there.

Zepp-LaRouche's call, made in 2007, to "Ban Violent Video Games" must be implemented before there are more "lone terrorist" incidents.

The release follows.

Helga Zepp-LaRouche: Ban Killer Video Games And Internet Violence!

December 10, 2007

Chairwoman of the Civil Rights Movement Solidarity (BüSo) in Germany, Helga Zepp-LaRouche, issued the statement below on Dec. 8, which has been translated from German.

Following the recent horrific news reports about young people running amok, killing their fellow students and teachers; young sharpshooters who knock off unknown victims; and young psychopathic murderers who kill other people after perverse film showings, all these incidents demonstrate in a dramatic way, how urgent it is to pass adequate laws to ban and place stiff penalties on the production and marketing of violence-glorifying computer games, as well as the use of the Internet to circulate violence-glorifying materials.

Finally, the Society for Scientific Discussion Psychotherapy (Gesellschaft für wissenschaftliche Gesprächpsychotherapie e.V., GwG), has come out with a demand for a total ban on these computer games. A representative of the society explained that "killer games are like land mines for the soul." And the GwG demands that politicians act, "before an entire generation of children and teenagers is sucked into a maelstrom of violence." Unfortunately, this is already happening.

Already in 1972, that is 35 years ago (!), the American Surgeon General, as well as the American Psychiatric Association, explained that there was an indisputable connection between violence in the media and violence committed by children and youth. And in virtually every case in which young people kill their fellow students and teachers with great precision in shooting, it turns out that there is an addiction to violent videos and to Internet sites that glorify violence. It is unfortunately the case, that the better part of two generations of children and teenagers have been exposed to the circulation of this mind- and soul-killing "entertainment."

The commercial killer videos had their origins in the military training programs, by means of which the U.S. Army used killing simulators to overcome the natural reluctance of soldiers to kill. The same thing happens with a video game, which makes killing a conditioned reflex.

The use of murder simulators for military training corresponds to the bestial concept of

PRNewsFoto/MICROSOFT

After standing in line for 24 hours, two video-game addicts (right) receive the first copies of Halo 3, in May 2007.

the Legionary Army, which was put forward by Samuel Huntington in his book *The Soldier and the State*, whereby soldiers are to be trained to carry out orders like zombies, who never challenge what they are told to do. If such a conception is barbaric in the army, then for children and youth, who are emotionally much more impressionable, it is an absolute catastrophe. The result is children and youth who are emotionally completely crippled, who can easily resort to aggression, and for whom the uniquely human capacity for feeling, and the ability to experience empathy, are completely absent. In the worst cases, they become autistic, or even murderers.

The EU Committee for "Human Rights in the Internet Society" is responsible for dealing with these issues, but has up until now failed to provide any effective guidelines for video games and Internet sites. If those who are in responsible positions fail to protect children and youth, they render themselves guilty of the violation of human rights. We demand an immediate ban on killer videos and an effective blockage of the aforementioned Internet sites!

INTERVIEW

Helga Zepp-LaRouche Addresses A World in Crisis

Tony Papert interviewed Helga Zepp-LaRouche on July 24.

Tony Papert: Helga Zepp-LaRouche is speaking to us from Germany, where she is engaged in far-reaching activity on a European and world scale. Helga, is the euro system about to break apart after last month's vote by the British to leave the European Union (EU)? Will that mean a world financial crash? Are there alternatives, and if so, what are they?

Helga Zepp-LaRouche: The Brexit is just one of several systemic crisis points. Naturally the Brexit's consequences are still very incalculable and represent a great risk to the financial system, but you also have the fact that the International Monetary Fund characterized Deutsche Bank as the bank most at risk in the international financial system. Deutsche Bank has an outstanding derivatives exposure of 55 trillion euro, while the GDP of the German economy is 4 trillion euro. The GDP of the EU is 18 trillion annually. Obviously, that bank alone has a derivatives exposure almost fourteen times the size of the entire German economy. That gives you a sense of how risk-loaded this bank really is.

But that is, in one sense, not a unique situation, be-cause all the major banks in Europe are totally under-capitalized, since the European governments and the international financial institutions have done nothing since 2008 to correct the casino economy; they have paid out three digit billions in dividends and profits, but they have not really moved to correct this completely crazy system in which, if one too-big-to-fail bank goes under, it will bring down, in a chain reaction, the whole financial system.

Then, on top of that, you have the Italian crisis, which has 360 billion euro in non-performing debt. Prime Minister Matteo Renzi has been desperately trying to get an exemption from the EU law which requires a bail-in, that is, the Cyprus model, which means the expropriation of the savers and those people who have bank stocks or bank bonds, as was done in Cyprus. This has already been applied four times in Italy with regional banks, with tremendous social consequences. Many people lost their life savings, there was even one suicide, and Renzi correctly fears a political revolt if he goes with the bail-in law.

On the other side, the EU and the German government know perfectly well that if Renzi is forced to implement the bail-in law anyway, this would almost certainly mean that he will lose the upcoming

CC/Università Ca' Foscari Venezia

Italian Prime Minister Matteo Renzi speaking at Università Ca' Foscari in Venice.

Cyprus residents protesting a bail-in, banks confiscating depositors' money, in 2013.

referendum on the Italian constitution in October, leading to new elections and bringing in, in all likelihood, the Five Star Party, which would take Italy out of the euro and probably out of the Eurozone—and that, for sure, would be the end of the EU and the euro.

So this is all a poker game with the lives and life savings of the population. We have been told by very well placed financial sources that the printing presses are running, because the so-called unorthodox monetary measures, meaning quantitative easing, meaning negative interest rates and so-called helicopter money,— all of that is not sufficient. They are printing physical bank-notes, cash, in case of emergency, and if it comes to this it will mean chaos; it will mean that a lot of people who spent their whole lives in honest work will lose everything, and this is where we are.

The Chilcot Report and the 28 Pages

Papert: During July in Britain, the Chilcot Report was released on Tony Blair's authorship or sponsorship of an illegal war in Iraq, and a few days later the long-classified 28 pages of the Joint Congressional 9/11 Inquiry, on Saudi responsibility for the 9/11 attacks, was released. Would you like to speak about the significance of these releases? You have long discussed the 28 pages of the 9/11 report.

Zepp-LaRouche: The 28 pages, which are now out with the exception of a few sentences that are still blacked out, simply make very clear that the entire history of 9/11 has to be re-written, because the role of Saudi financing of Wahhabi, Salafist terrorism is very,

very clear. Recall that a little more than a week ago there was a horrible massacre in Nice, which was the fifth major terrorist attack in France since the beginning of 2015. But at the time of the first of these incidents—the massacre at the offices of *Charlie Hebdo*—former U.S. Senator Bob Graham said that that terrorist attack would not have occurred if these 28 pages had been published, and obviously that is still the case. In other words, we need a full investigation of the implications in these 28 pages for the emergence of the phenomena of international terrorism.

Now, the Chilcot Report gives the aftermath, or the consequences of what happened after 9/11, namely the wars based on lies, against Iraq, Afghanistan, Libya, and Syria. Obviously Saddam Hussein was not involved with Al-Qaida. We knew that at the time, because he used to put clerics in jail. He was a secular person, and we knew that any link to Al-Qaida was a lie. We knew it was a lie that Saddam Hussein had weapons of mass destruction.

It is very clear that the Chilcot Report is the follow-up story of the 28 pages. Therefore, the two documents must be seen as one, in one context, and must be investigated, because elements of these two documents have all kinds of international implications, including the Afghanistan war, where Article 5 of NATO was invoked. I think it requires that there be an investigation in all countries affected by the content of these two documents.

The 'New Violence'

Papert: Our interview occurs in the immediate aftermath of the killings in Würzburg and Munich, Germany. What is the answer to these sorts of killings, and in particular, how should Americans understand them and work to end them?

Zepp-LaRouche: It is very interesting that, in contrast to Nice, where there was clearly a connection with Islamic terrorism, the murders or terrorist incidents in Würzburg and especially Munich, had everything to do with "amok" attacks. In fact, the culprit in the Munich

A snapshot from a killer video game.

case had chosen that day as the fifth anniversary of the Breivik horror show in Norway five years ago; the anniversary was on that day. German Interior Minister [Thomas] de Maiziere said afterwards that the harmful effects of killer video games on young people cannot be doubted.

My husband, Lyndon LaRouche, started a campaign against the "new violence" at the beginning of 2000, and I gave a speech to an audience at the São Paulo State Appellate Criminal Court in Brazil in 2002, in which I went into the history of how these violent video games had developed out of military training to increase the kill rate, because people had found that, among soldiers in World War II, only 15% of soldiers in World War II were even willing to shoot at the enemy, because human beings have a built-in hesitance to kill other members of their kind. The video games were developed to increase the kill rate in the army, and only after that were they developed to become commercial video games.

I, at that time, demanded an international outlawing and banning of these video games, including blocking them on the Internet. That was pooh-poohed at that time, with people saying, "Oh, you can't block the Internet." This is a complete lie. Now everybody is com-pletely hysterical about the fact that China is very effectively blocking entire parts of the Internet, so it can be done. But now, when terrorism is completely out of control, all aspects of it, now is the time to renew this demand to outlaw these kinds of satanic video games.

At the same time, terrorism has totally gotten out of control. In the recent period—the last year and a half—more than 30 countries on four continents have been hit by terrorism, some countries almost every week. For example, Kabul, yesterday another 80 people killed; Baghdad,— these people are suffering as much from these terrorist attacks as the people in Nice or Paris, or Munich, except that the international media choose not to report it. This thing is out of control, and therefore it is absolutely crucial to take up the proposal of President Putin at the 2015 UN General Assembly, offering international cooperation to fight terrorism. Anybody who does not pick up on that proposal is implicitly complicit in all future such terrorist attacks.

Deutsche Bank

Papert: You, with Lyndon LaRouche, your husband, have launched a campaign to re-organize and re-orient Deutsche Bank. Could you speak about that?

Xinhua/Khalil Dawood

A firefighter at the scene of a car bomb attack in the Karrada-Kakhil district of southern Baghdad, Iraq, July 3, 2016.

Zepp-LaRouche: The question is, what can you do to prevent the pending disaster of a disorderly financial disintegration of the financial system? Obviously it is very good that Glass-Steagall is now in the platform of both the Democratic and Republican parties, which is a major breakthrough, and it has a lot to do with the work of our organization in particular, but it is a long way from the platform to legislation by Congress and the Senate, and that is what is urgently needed.

That is why what we propose is to use the fact that Deutsche Bank is in a critical condition to say, Okay, there was a time when the business plan of Deutsche Bank was completely different,

Alfred Herrhausen

namely in the period when Alfred Herrhausen was the head of the bank. He was probably the last moral banker with integrity in Europe, for whom morality and banking were not in contradiction.

We are still involved in this campaign; we have gotten a lot of very interested responses in many countries on both sides of the Atlantic, and an interesting reflection may be that, according to rumors at the end of last week, around Friday, Deutsche Bank itself is apparently moving away from its position of being a universal bank, and is considering separating its different economic functions within the bank itself. In other words, to separate the commercial bank making loans to industry,— separating that completely from the investment branch.

I would say that this is a remarkable admission that the universal banking system doesn't function, and we have to see how this plays out. Obviously, without getting rid of the casino aspect of the entire monetary system, it will not be sufficient, but I think it is interesting that people are starting to think in this way. We will, for sure, continue this discussion, because it is very urgent, and the reform of Deutsche Bank in the way we propose it is one way to get at the meat of the matter.

The Berlin Conference

Papert: You led an international conference in Berlin last month, which was featured in *EIR*. What is the message of the conference for the ongoing crisis which you have just described in depth?

Zepp-LaRouche: We really wanted to make clear that this is a civilizational crisis which has a strategic component involving the immediate war danger because of—among other things— the aggressive NATO expansion to the Russian border, the situation in the Middle East, the situation in the South China Sea, the already mentioned financial crisis, and many other aspects of what we call a civilizational crisis. You do not get out of this by cosmetic reforms here and there. The purpose of the conference in Berlin was to convey the message that we need to have an entirely new paradigm.

The new paradigm must supersede geopolitics, and that is why we are promoting the New Silk Road, proposed by China's President Xi Jinping three years ago, to become the World Land-Bridge, in other words, to become a program of reconstruction of the entire world economy. It is very clear that that is feasible.

It is very easy to extend the Silk Road into the Middle East, Southwest Asia, and Africa, and in that way also to solve the refugee crisis, because many millions of people are fleeing from war, hunger, and epidemics, and there must be a new perspective of working together of all major nations on this planet—Russia, China, India, the United States, European nations. If they all joined hands and said, "We will develop Asia and Africa," you could really solve any problem in the world, and obviously this must be combined with a cultural renaissance, because if you do not uplift the thinking of the people, nothing will be accomplished.

This is why the Berlin conference had, besides very concrete economic proposals, also a very beautiful concert on the basis of the dialogue of cultures, in which we tried to represent the highest expression of different cultures—Chinese, Russian, European. That dialogue of the highest spirit of what humankind has produced has to be reactivated, and has to be the basis for a coming Renaissance. So, this Berlin conference was simply a way to show how easy it would be to bring the world into order if people are motivated by good will.

Glass-Steagall—Then and Now

by Robert Ingraham

July 25—It is sometimes said that since the events of September 11, 2001, society, politics, and security concerns have all been radically transformed by the events and aftermath of that day, such that we are all now living within a new paradigm, designated as the "post-9/11" world. The Patriot Act, unprecedented levels of warrantless government spying, ongoing permanent warfare, and seemingly non-stop incidents of terrorism and mass killing have all become commonplace in this new reality.

To simply confine the definition of this new paradigm to the realm of military and related spheres, however, would be a critical mistake. It must also be remembered that 18 months, to the day, prior to the 9/11 attacks, the repeal of Franklin Roosevelt's Glass-Steagall Act went into effect on March 11, 2000. Since that day, we have been living in a *post-Glass-Steagall world,* and all of the ensuing events and developments since March 11, 2000 and Sept. 11, 2001 must be seen as two components of one unified unfolding process.

The repeal of Glass-Steagall was not merely a legislative act. It was accomplished only after a more than ten-year process, a bloody process which included the assassination of the German Deutsche Bank Chairman Alfred Herrhausen, the impeachment of the President of the United States, the imprisonment of Lyndon LaRouche, and the near annihilation of his organization. The destruction of Glass-Steagall opened the door for an unprecedented seizure of power by the London-Wall Street financial interests, the same interests who then unleashed a still ongoing dynamic of permanent warfare throughout the planet, a dynamic which is now leading directly toward a strategic confrontation with Russia and China. It is precisely the underlying importance of this financial and banking crisis that motivated Helga Zepp-LaRouche to issue the statement "Deutsche Bank Must Be Saved, for the Sake of World Peace!" on July 12, 2016.

The Present Opportunity

On July 18, 2016, the Republican National Convention, meeting in Cleveland, voted as a body to demand the immediate re-enactment of Glass-Steagall legislation. That vote has sent shock-waves through the corridors of power and elicited horrified reactions from Wall Street stooges, both in New York City and Washington, D.C.

The pre-platform of the Democratic Party also contains a pro-Glass-Steagall plank, and expectations are high that when its convention meets on July 25, the full

U.S. Navy/Mass Comm. Spc. 2nd Class Julio Rivera

In what has become common place in the post-9/11 world, Marines board the assault ship USS Bataan, March 2011, for deployment to the Libyan coast to participate in overthrowing the government.

body will also endorse a return to Glass-Steagall.

Thus, for the first time since 1999, we find ourselves at a moment where both of the major U.S. political parties are in the process of placing themselves, on record, calling for a return to Glass-Steagall.

None of these developments came about through accident. It was in the midst of the global financial crisis in 2008 that Lyndon LaRouche, in a video broadcast, issued the call for the immediate re-imposition of Glass-Steagall measures, and it has been the LaRouche PAC, during the last eight years, which has spearheaded this effort, garnering support from hundreds of elected officials, European and other foreign dignitaries, and many influential policy-makers and leaders. Over 600,000 American citizens signed a LaRouche PAC-circulated petition calling for a return to Glass-Steagall.

U.S. Army

The scene of the assassination of Alfred Herrhausen.

This fight reached a milestone in 2011, when Ohio Congresswoman Marcy Kaptur introduced into the U.S. House of Representatives, H.R.1489, the Return to Prudent Banking Act, legislation which would re-enact the Glass-Steagall Act of 1933. Since that date, a number of different bills have been introduced into every session of the U.S. Congress, with the 2013 legislation gaining 83 co-sponsors, and the current bill, H.R.381, already having more than 70 co-sponsors.

The Actual Glass-Steagall Battle

Even a cursory examination of current discussion of Glass-Steagall on the Internet reveals that there is, at present, an enormous amount of discussion on the issue. For a select few among Wall Street leaders, the full implications are known—and feared. For many others, however, Glass-Steagall is still too often discussed and understood as only a matter of banking "reform," essentially a measure seen as correcting certain "abuses" within the financial community. The profound implications of what is at stake are simply not comprehended.

To grasp the full import of this battle, it is necessary to go back to 1989, to the period of the fall of the Berlin Wall, and the decisions that were made at that time by the British Empire, its puppet Mitterrand's France, and the U.S. Bush Administration.

In January 1989, prior to the fall of the Wall, Lyndon LaRouche, together with many of his closest associates, were imprisoned in the United States. As subsequent events would show, this action—to "remove LaRouche from the scene"—was an essential prerequisite for the successful designs of London and Wall Street.

The Berlin Wall fell in November 1989. Deutsche Bank Chairman Alfred Herrhausen was scheduled to deliver a speech in New York City on Dec. 4, 1989, a speech in which he would call for a Marshall-Plan-type approach for western investment in Eastern Europe, modeled on the practice of the German *Kreditanstalt für Wiederaufbau,* for massive investment in industry, manufacturing and infrastructure (see *EIR*, Vol. 43, No. 30, July 22, 2016). Herrhausen was also an outspoken advocate of Third World debt forgiveness and global physical economic investment. Four days before Herrhausen was scheduled to deliver this speech, on Nov. 30, 1989, he was assassinated in a very sophisticated professional attack, and his murderers remain unidentified to this day.

In the same month that Herrhausen was assassinated, Lyndon LaRouche, from his prison cell, issued his proposal for the creation of a European "Productive Triangle." Fully coherent with Herrhausen's design for advanced industrial and technological development in Eastern Europe, LaRouche's proposal would then be published in January 1990 as "The Productive Triangle, Paris-Berlin-Vienna: Locomotive for the World Economy."

The killing of Herrhausen and the subsequent imposition of "financial shock and awe" against Russia, designed to utterly destroy that nation, then proceeded in tandem with the drive for a full Wall Street policy dictatorship within the United States, the key component of which was the abolition of Glass-Steagall.

Earlier, in 1987, the Ayn Rand cultist Alan Greenspan had already been appointed as Chairman of the U.S. Federal Reserve, and then, in 1988, Wendy Gramm, the wife of Senator Phil Gramm—who one year later would author the bill to repeal Glass-Steagall—was named Chairman of the Commodity Futures Trading Commission (CFTC), an organization created in 1974 by the Nixon Administration. Under Gramm's leadership, the CFTC exceeded its authority in several actions to bring about further deregulation of banking and financial markets. Under the leadership of Greenspan and Wendy Gramm, a non-stop campaign was launched, which escalated throughout the 1980s, to remove all government oversight over banking and the financial markets and to transform the banking system into one giant speculative gambling operation. Although the motives of Greenspan and his ilk may have simply been delusional, for the actual controllers of the Empire, this was all about power and domination, not simply financial looting.

In 1998 the trap was set when Citicorp and the Travelers Group announced to the world that they had merged, creating "Citigroup," becoming at that time the largest financial corporation in the world. Under the provisions of Glass-Steagall, this merger was illegal, since Glass-Steagall prohibited banks from merging with insurance underwriters. The Citicorp/Travelers announcement was

Das „produktive Dreieck"
Paris – Berlin – Wien

Lokomotive der Weltwirtschaft

— Schiller-Institut —

A map of the productive triangle, from Paris to Berlin to Vienna, the industrial area proposed by Lyndon LaRouche as a locomotive to the world economy.

Former Federal Reserve Chairman Alan Greenspan testifying to Congress.

a de facto challenge to the authority and sovereignty of the U.S. government, posing the question, "who exactly is in charge" of American economic and financial policy? In 1999 Senator Phil Gramm announced his intention to repeal Glass-Steagall, and in November of that year, the Gramm-Leach-Bliley Act was passed, with the strong support of Alan Greenspan and the pro-Wall Street grouping around Vice-President Gore in the Executive Branch. It took effect 120 days later, thus abolishing the entirety of the Glass-Steagall provisions.

Seeing the Larger Context

During the period of 1990 through 1995, led by Helga Zepp-LaRouche, the Schiller Institute conducted an aggressive worldwide campaign on behalf of the principles and economic initiatives contained in the Productive Triangle proposal. This led into the 1992 Eurasian Landbridge proposal, which expanded the original concept into one which included the entirety of the former Soviet territories in Russia and central Asia, stretching all the way to the Pacific coast of China. Later, at a 1994 conference in Eltville, Germany, in which Lyndon LaRouche was able to personally take part for the first time since his imprisonment, this perspective was further refined by Mrs. LaRouche as the "New Silk Road" project, whose effects we continue to see unfold in the present day.

The Asian Financial Crisis of 1997-1998 and the collapse of Long Term Capital Management in September 1998 brought matters to a head. On the one side, on Feb. 17, 1997, the Schiller Institute, under the direction of Lyndon and Helga LaRouche, issued an appeal to U.S. Pres-

courtesy of the William J. Clinton Library

President William Clinton signs the Gramm-Leach-Bliley Act on Nov. 12, 1999, which removed the separation between investment banking and commercial banks that had been the law of the land since the 1933 Glass-Stegall Act of President Franklin Roosevelt.

ident Bill Clinton, calling on him to convoke a New Bretton Woods Conference for the purpose of monetary reform. Within weeks this appeal was endorsed by dozens of leading political figures from throughout the world, including former presidents from Mexico, Brazil, and Uganda.

An intense policy debate emerged within the Clinton Administration. In the opening weeks of 1998, U.S. Treasury Secretary Robert Rubin spoke of an urgent need to devise "a new architecture." Rubin also stated repeatedly that he "would not spend a nickel to 'bail out' failing, bankrupt speculators and banks." This potential policy shift was also echoed in Senate Bill 1769, the Clinton Administration's "1998 Supplemental Appropriations Act for the International Monetary Fund." Although this bill increased IMF spending authority, it tied any increase to the creation of a Presidential Advisory Commission to review the "future role . . . if any" of the IMF, and mandated the convening of a "New Bretton Woods Conference" within 180 days. Finally, on Sept. 14, 1998, President Clinton delivered a speech to the Council on Foreign Relations in New York City where he was explicit in his call for a "new financial architecture."

The response of the financial oligarchy to these developments was two-fold: First, to move immediately for Bill Clinton's impeachment and his removal from office; second, to escalate the drive for the full abolition of Glass-Steagall.

Bill Clinton's involvement with Monica Lewinsky occurred in 1995 and 1996, but it was not until Linda Tripp handed over recordings of her telephone conversations with Lewinsky to Kenneth Starr in January 1998 that the legal targeting of Clinton went into high gear. For almost the entirety of 1998, and continuing until his acquittal by the Senate on Feb. 12, 1999, Bill Clinton was under siege in a manner almost unprecedented in U.S. history. Despite his eventual acquittal, this process, including the Dec. 19, 1998 votes of 228-206 and 221-212 by the full House of Representatives to impeach Clinton on two counts, essentially destroyed the Clinton Presidency.

Nine months after Clinton's acquittal by the U.S. Senate, both houses of Congress voted to pass the Gramm-Leach-Bliley Act repealing Glass-Steagall. The act took effect in March 2000, and later in that December, Congress enacted the Commodity Futures Modernization Act, which both legalized Over the Counter (OTC) speculative derivatives trading, effectively opening the floodgates for the emergence of the financial casino which exists today, and simultaneously vastly reducing the oversight powers of the Securities and Exchange Commission.

Nine months later, two planes piloted by British/ Saudi-sponsored terrorists struck the World Trade Center.

The Financial Security State

Some have dubbed the 20th Century as "a century of war." If that appellation is true, then the 21st Century, up until now, can only be understood as the last bloodthirsty stand of the British-London imperial financial system. And properly understood, this imperial grab for absolute power, this new 21st Century paradigm, began in 1998 and 1999 with the impeachment of the sitting U.S. President and the abolition of Franklin Roosevelt's Glass-Steagall policy.

The key thing to grasp in all of this is that which is axiomatic, not the specifics or all of the details. A British Empire *coup d'etat* was carried out within the United States from 1998 to 2001, placing the London-allied Wall Street interests in control of our government. All of the wars, the terrorism, the suffering, and the deaths of the last fifteen years stem from these developments, and now we are witnessing these same interests move towards a nuclear showdown with both Russia and China, attempting to "bluff" those nations into kowtowing to the demands of London and Wall Street.

The post-9/11 passage of the Patriot Act, the massive expansion of government spying and the military trappings of the "war on terrorism" all must be seen within this context. The TARP bailout of 2008, and the even more staggering Citigroup bailout of that year, are indicators of the fascist-type apparatus which has been created by George W. Bush and Barack Obama. As we move toward the November U.S. Presidential election, frantic efforts are now being made by the U.S. Federal Reserve and its allies at the Bank of England and the European Central Bank, in the form of "helicopter money," to try to stave off their own financial collapse, regardless of the lunacy of such actions, and regardless of the effects on either the populations of these nations or the precarious balance of war and peace in the world.

Action … And Action Now!

It would be the height of foolishness to believe that, simply because of the current Democratic and Republican platforms, there is a guarantee that either Hillary Clinton or Donald Trump will seriously challenge the paradigm of the last sixteen years, or that either of them will act to restore Glass-Steagall. Nevertheless, the current crisis is severe and worsening by the day. The solution—the pathway out—was indicated by Lyndon LaRouche in his proposal for taking a Hamiltonian approach to saving the now desperate Deutsche Bank.

EIRNS/Robert Wesser

LaRouche PAC activists rally to revive Hamilton's program at Federal Hall, Manhattan, on July 16, 2015.

The inclusion of pro-Glass-Steagall planks in the platforms of both the Republican and Democratic parties is an indicator of the potential which exists in the near term for a fundamental shift in policy. Glass-Steagall, and all that it implies, is now fully part of the national policy debate. To succeed in this fight, however, will require that greater numbers of people reach a full realization of the manner whereby Glass-Steagall was destroyed. In that context, the recent revelations of the Chilcot Commission in regard to the Iraq War, and the U.S. decision to release the 28 pages on Saudi involvement in 9/11 may play a pivotal liberating role in helping people to understand what transpired during this period.

Only then can we get beyond impotent dead-end discussion of "banking reform." The Russians and the Chinese are offering full partnership with the United States in both a real War on Terrorism as well as in the economic development projects of the New Silk Road. What is required is a revolution in thinking in the United States, a true return to an actual Hamiltonian economic approach. Perhaps, if people understand what was done to them, and why it was done, the needed changes might be accomplished.

After Terrorist Attacks, Cooperation With Russia Is Even More Urgent

by Helga Zepp-LaRouche

The author is chairwoman of the German political party Civil Rights Movement Solidarity (BüSo).

July 23—While France has been hit by five horrendous terror attacks since the beginning of 2015, and brutal attacks have occurred in the same time frame in more than 30 countries (often more than once) in Europe, Asia, the United States, and Africa—the reality of the terrorist threat has now been experienced firsthand in Germany, with the attacks in Würzburg and Munich,[1] whatever the biography or description of the perpetrators turns out to be (whether political Islamists or "self-radicalized" lone assassins). Without a doubt, the problem of international terrorism is one of the major threats to humanity as a whole.

In a situation in which a whole array of crises is coming on thick and fast—the growing war danger in Europe, Southwest Asia, and the Pacific; an attempted coup and subsequent consolidation of state power in Turkey, a NATO state; Brexit and the erosion of the European Union; and a new imminent financial crisis, to name only a few—it should be obvious that we can only solve these crises if we discard the old ways of thinking and geopolitical rancors, and if the most important states work together on an international level.

CSU parliamentarian Hans-Peter Uhl was right, in the wake of the night of horror in Munich, to call for improved, preventive measures and heightened cooperation among the relevant authorities, both domestically and abroad. But given the history and international operating mode of radical Islam, that obviously implies cooperation with Russia, the victim that has the most expertise on the networks in Chechnya and their

UN photo/Cia Pak

Russian President Vladimir Putin addressing the seventieth session of the UN General Assembly, Sept. 28, 2015, in which he called for collaboration among nations to deal with terrorism.

links to the Right Sector in Ukraine and to ISIS, and which has proven, through its military intervention in Syria, to be the only country that has successfully pushed back the power of ISIS.

It is therefore urgent to take up the offer extended by President Vladimir Putin in his speech to the UN General Assembly in 2015. After pointing to the fatal consequences of the West's policy of training allegedly "moderate" rebels to combat secular governments in the Middle East, who then defected in droves to ISIS, Putin stressed:

> In these circumstances, it is hypocritical and irresponsible to make declarations about the threat of terrorism, and at the same time turn a blind eye to the channels used to finance and support terrorists, including revenues from drug trafficking, the illegal oil trade, and the arms trade.
>
> It is equally irresponsible to manipulate extremist groups and use them to achieve your political goals, hoping that later you'll find a way to get rid of them or somehow eliminate them....

---

1. Nine Germans were massacred in a Munich shopping area on July 22 by an 18-year-old German-Iranian. The attack came just days after a 17-year-old Afghan refugee attacked and wounded passengers with an axe, on a train in the city of Würzburg.

NATO photo

Former UK Prime Minister Tony Blair (left) next to then President George W. Bush at a NATO summit meeting in Istanbul, Turkey, June 29, 2004, less than a year after Blair's lies about Iraq were used as a pretext by Bush to start the war against Iraq in 2003.

What we actually propose is to be guided by common values and common interests rather than by ambitions. Relying on international law, we must join efforts to address the problem that all of us are facing, and create a genuinely broad international coalition against terrorism. Similar to the anti-Hitler coalition, it could unite a broad range of parties willing to stand firm against those who, just like the Nazis, sow evil and hatred of humankind. And of course, Muslim nations should play a key role in such a coalition, since Islamic State not only poses a direct threat to them, but also tarnishes one of the greatest world religions with its atrocities. The ideologues of these extremists make a mockery of Islam and subvert its true humanist values. [Kremlin translation]

Especially since the newly released Chilcot Inquiry report in Great Britain spotlights how Tony Blair orchestrated the war of aggression against Iraq on the basis of conscious lies, and the disclosure of the suppressed 28 pages of the official Joint Congressional Inquiry into 9/11 has left no doubt as to the role of Saudi Arabia in financing ter-

rorism, a "more of the same" policy is tantamount to complicity in any new terrorist attacks.

The German authorities can no longer hide behind the usual sociological sophisms. The credibility of Mr. Uhl and Interior Minister Thomas de Mazière, of the members of the Bundestag's domestic affairs committee, and of course of Chancellor Merkel, will depend on whether they initiate an official investigation to elucidate as quickly as possible the implications of these two documents—the Chilcot Report and the 28 pages—and draw the conclusions from them. It is unacceptable, under any circumstances, to use the attacks in Würzburg and Munich as the excuse to build up a police state as Turkish President Erdogan is doing, and to cooperate with precisely those governments that are exposed and implicated by the Chilcot Report and the 28 pages.

The Next Financial Crisis: Italy

A dramatic change in policy is also urgently necessary with respect to another existential crisis, the financial one. The word is out everywhere that Italy is the new Greece. But unlike Greece, it doesn't represent just two percent of the European Union's GDP, but is the fourth largest industrial nation in Europe. Yet the European Commission, the European Central Bank (ECB), and the German Finance Ministry are pursuing the same brutal and incompetent policy which has already ruined Greece and eroded the European Union (EU). Italy's GDP has shrunk by about 25 percent as a result

EC Audiovisual Service/Etienne Ansotte

From left: Christine Lagarde, Managing Director the IMF; Jean-Claude Juncker, EU Commission President; Mario Draghi, President of the European Central Bank (ECB); and French President François Hollande. They agree that savers and investors should pay for rescue of the sick banks in Italy, as they were in Cyprus.

Anti-austerity protests in Italy send a message to Prime Minister Matteo Renzi.

of the EU's murderous austerity policy since the 2008 financial crisis, leading to horrible consequences for the healthcare system and pensions, an increase in unemployment, the shutdown of many small and medium-sized businesses, and a dramatic rise in suicides. One result of this shrinking of the real economy by about one quarter is that the Italian banks are now sitting on 360 billion euros of non-performing loans.

The medicine that ECB head Mario Draghi, EU Commission President Jean-Claude Juncker, the Bundesbank, and German Finance Minister Wolfgang Schäuble intend to administer to the "sick man of Europe," is poisonous. They all agree, with minimal differences, that Italian savers and investors should pay for the rescue of the sick banks, as the EU's bail-in law prescribes, thus accepting the Cyprus model—in the event that the stress test results for the Italian banks, to be made public at the end of July, show—as expected—that these banks are undercapitalized.

In that case, Italian savers and investors would have their money expropriated, and Prime Minister Matteo Renzi, as a result, would be threatened with a revolt. He would most likely lose the upcoming referendum for constitutional reform in October and he would lose the subsequent elections. The Five Star Movement would then set in motion Italy's exit from the euro and the European Union.

While various media, among them *Die Welt*, describe Italy as a "failed state," putting it for all intents and purposes in the same category as Somalia or Iraq, the so-called EU political leadership is doing nothing—absolutely nothing—to remedy the crisis. What these soulless EU bureaucrats such as Juncker, ECB head Draghi, and other politicians and bankers who have made their careers by passing through the revolving door between politics and the major banking houses several times, have not for one moment taken into account, is that their policies in support of the casino economy are ruining entire nations, the lives and fortunes of many millions of people.

The Solution

There is a solution: The *Büso* is working with many collaborators in Europe and the United States in a campaign to avert the threatened insolvency of Deutsche Bank through a return to the banking philosophy which underlay the policy of the assassinated chairman of the bank, Alfred Herrhausen.[2] This campaign has generated a good deal of attention from the financial sector, since everyone knows that the trans-Atlantic financial system is hopelessly bankrupt. In this context, the report that Deutsche Bank is preparing for an in-house separation of its business and investment sections, is of interest.

The fact that the demand for a return to the Glass-Steagall banking separation law has been incorporated into the party platforms of both the Democratic and Republican parties—the result of many years of campaigning by the LaRouche Political Action Committee—has so far had two interesting results: It has produced screams from Wall Street, which fears Glass-Steagall more than the devil fears holy water, and it has discredited all those who constantly claimed that it couldn't be done.

In these turbulent days there is a simple measure at hand, which will allow anyone to see whether leading politicians are championing the general welfare of the people they are supposed to represent, or whether they are lobbyists for other interests. This measure is their readiness to seize the existing solutions—that is, to accept Putin's offer, and to return to an economic policy based on serving the general welfare. Politicians who fail to measure up should be hounded out of office for just that reason.

---

2. "Webcast with Zepp-LaRouche: Bank Rescue Plan Is Last Chance," *EIR*, July 22, 2016, pp. 5-20.

Every Day Counts In Today's Showdown To Save Civilization

That's why you need EIR's **Daily Alert Service**, a strategic overview compiled with the input of Lyndon LaRouche, and delivered to your email 5 days a week.

For example: On Jan. 7, EIR's Daily Alert featured the British hand behind the pattern of global provocations toward war. Of special note is British Intelligence's role in instigating the Saudi Kingdom's attempt to set off a Sunni-Shia war. This religious war has been the intent of British strategy since the Blair-Bush attack on Iraq in 2003.

We also uniquely update you regularly on the progress toward the release of the suppressed 28 pages of the Congressional Inquiry on 9/11, which would expose the Saudi role.

Every edition highlights the reality of the impending financial crash/bail-in policies that would realize the British goal of mass depopulation.

This is intelligence you need to act on, if we are going to survive as a nation and a species. Can you really afford to be without it?

THURSDAY, JANUARY 7, 2016

Volume 2, Number 97

EIR Daily Alert Service

P.O. Box 17390, Washington, DC 20041-0390

- British Crown Pushing War and Genocide in 2016
- Financial Mudslide Goes On; Monetarist Tyranny Gloats over Bail-Ins
- Moody's Downgrades Portugal's Novo Banco
- Puerto Rico's Default: It's Every Vulture for Himself
- Wide Glass-Steagall Debate Set Off Again by Sanders Speech
- MI6 Mouthpiece Evans-Pritchard Touts Persian Gulf Chaos
- North Korea Tests a Miniaturized Hydrogen Bomb
- Uighur Terrorists Found in Indonesia
- Foreign Investors Are Flocking In to China

EDITORIAL

British Crown Pushing War and Genocide in 2016

III. Their Time Is Over

THEIR TIME IS UP

The Chilcot Report and the 28 Pages

by Jeffrey Steinberg

July 27—The July 6 publication of the Chilcot Commission report in Britain, followed nine days later by the release of the 28-page suppressed chapter of the original Joint Congressional Inquiry into 9/11 of December 2002, is a watershed that must now lead to the dismantling of the British Empire. Taken together, the two documents are a clear indictment of the policies that have dominated the Anglo-American sphere for the last decade and a half, beginning with the Sept. 11, 2001 attacks on the Pentagon and the World Trade Center.

The Chilcot Investigation: 2009-2016

Sir John Chilcot was appointed to head an independent investigation into Britain's role in the events from 2001 to 2009, spanning the 9/11 attacks, the joint Anglo-American invasion of Iraq in March 2003, and the events that followed. The appointment was announced on June 15, 2009 by Prime Minister Gordon Brown, who named Sir John Chilcot to head the five-person Privy Council Commission.

When the Privy Counsellors' Report was made public on July 6, 2016, it comprised 12 volumes of more than 6,000 pages, with 2.6 million words. The Executive Summary alone was 145 pages, with 911 separate itemized findings of fact, all condemning the entire war scheme.

Chilcot issued a statement

White House photo/David Bohrer

Vice President Dick Cheney speaking with British Prime Minister Tony Blair before departing London March 11, 2002, a year before the Blair-orchestrated invasion of Iraq carried out by the George W. Bush Administration.

moments prior to the release, in which he summarized the findings. It was nothing short of a stunning indictment of Tony Blair and his American partners, George W. Bush and Dick Cheney, for going to war before exhausting all of the available diplomatic options, for misrepresenting the actual intelligence to obtain public consent for the invasion and overthrow of Saddam Hussein's government, and for failing to prepare for the aftermath of the invasion.

Chilcot reported that, although Blair initially cautioned President Bush against taking "hasty action" in Iraq, Blair himself had abandoned any such caution by April 2002, when he traveled to Crawford, Texas to confer with Bush. By that time, the British Joint Intelligence Committee had concluded that "Saddam Hussein could not be removed without an invasion."

While the world media had characterized Tony Blair as George Bush's "poodle," loyally following Bush on the path to war, the Chilcot findings were that the British were driving every key decision, from the launching of invasion plans even prior to the April 2002 Crawford war council, to the decision to take the Iraq issue to the United Nations on Sept. 7, 2002, to the issuing of the Sept. 24, 2002 "dodgy dossier" which was used by both Washington and London to make the fraudulent case that

President George W. Bush and British Prime Minister speaking at a joint press conference May 2, 2002, after meeting in Crawford, Texas. The meeting was referred to as the Crawford War Council.

Saddam Hussein was stockpiling and concealing a huge "weapons of mass destruction" inventory and secret research program.

Chilcot also made clear, in his presentation of the Privy Council investigation's findings, that the post-invasion catastrophe was not "unknowable," as Blair claimed after the fact. "The risks of internal strife in Iraq, active Iranian pursuit of its interests, regional instability, and Al-Qaeda activity in Iraq, were each explicitly identified before the invasion," he told reporters July 6.

The Commission concluded that the consequences of the British and American invasion included at least 150,000 Iraqi deaths, "most of them civilians," and the displacing of more than one million Iraqis.

Many of the thousands of documents included in the report, and the Commission's own findings, exposed the active hand of Prime Minister Blair in bypassing any parliamentary oversight, in pursuit of a war in violation of the Nuremberg Code and the United Nations Charter, which ban aggressive war as a crime against humanity. Over 170 British soldiers and more than 2,000 American soldiers have been killed in the Iraq War so far. Families of the British soldiers who gave their lives in the illegal war are now suing Tony Blair—and they have called for the convening of a United Nations tribunal at the International Court of Justice, to try Blair, Bush, and Cheney for their war crimes.

The 28 Pages

After a 14-year battle, faced with a growing public demand, led by a powerful coalition of current and former elected officials, and survivors and family members of the 2,997 innocent people killed in the Sept. 11, 2001 attacks, and with the LaRouche Political Action Committee's "Manhattan Project" in a key role, President Barack Obama relented on July 15 and approved the declassification of the partially redacted 28-page chapter of the December 2002 report of the Joint Congressional Inquiry.

As to the timing of the release, it is clear that the press conference of Representatives Walter Jones (R-N.C.), Stephen Lynch (D-Mass.), and Thomas Massie (R-Ky.) on July 6, 2016 finally forced the issue. In this press conference, they vowed to make the suppressed chapter public, even if it required invoking the "Gravel Option" of publicly revealing the content of the 28 pages from the floor of the House.

While President Obama, his CIA Director John Brennan, and the Saudi Royal Family attempted, in vain, once the pages were made public, to claim that the 28 pages "vindicated" the Saudis and showed no direct

One plane of many that returned from Iraq, loaded with flag-draped coffins.

involvement in the worst terrorist attacks on U.S. soil in history, no sane person reading the released pages could ignore the massive evidence of a direct Saudi government hand in the creation and building up of Al-Qaeda, and in providing direct, material support to some of the 9/11 hijackers.

But a larger context reveals an even more hideous truth: President George W. Bush suppressed the publication of the 28 pages in December 2002, at the height of the U.S. and British preparations for the invasion of Iraq and the overthrow of Saddam Hussein. Had those 28 pages been included in the published version of the report of the Joint Inquiry at that time, it would have been impossible for Bush and Blair to go forward with their long-established Iraq invasion plans.

The assault on Iraq, which began March 19-20, 2003, was premised on two Big Lies: First, that Saddam Hussein had an arsenal of weapons of mass destruction; and second, that Saddam Hussein had a hand in 9/11.

Had the 28 pages—showing damning evidence of Saudi support for the 9/11 hijackers—been released to the American public and the world when they were written in December 2002, an invasion of Iraq would have been the moral equivalent of bombing China, instead of Japan, following the attack on Pearl Harbor on Dec. 7, 1941.

9/11 'Reichstag Fire' —An Inside Job

From top to bottom, the overwhelming evidence, assembled by the Joint Inquiry staff under enormous limitations, made clear that all trails pointed to Saudi Arabia as the sponsors and pa-

georgewbush-whitehouse.archives.gov
President Bush and Vice President Dick Cheney en route to a motorcade taking them to 9/11 memorial ceremony at the Pentagon.

Image from Iraqi state television
Saddam Hussein on election day, Oct. 16, 2002, five months before the invasion of Iraq.

trons of the 9/11 attack. As the direct result of 9/11, George Bush and Dick Cheney brought the United States to war, ripped up major portions of the U.S. Constitution through measures like the Patriot Act, and bankrupted the United States through a war effort that has, so far, cost taxpayers an estimated $3 trillion—while granting tax cuts to the super-rich at the same time.

In January 2001, Lyndon LaRouche had publicly warned that the Bush-Cheney Administration would move to create a "Reichstag Fire" incident to provide the pretext for ripping up the U.S. Constitution. The Bush Administration's two closest allies, Great Britain and Saudi Arabia, were both implicated in the crime of 9/11, and as the events were unfolding on September 11, 2001, Lyndon LaRouche told a radio audience that such a coordinated attack was not possible without some "inside help."

Anglo-Saudi Partnership for Terrorism

The 28-page chapter from the Joint Inquiry forms a compelling part of the narrative assembled by the Chilcot Commission. By early 2001, Great Britain was already the target of diplomatic protests from governments around the globe for its protection and financing of terrorist organizations. In 1999, the Russian government fired off a series of diplomatic *démarches* over flagrant British protection of Chechen terrorists who, in some cases, were being given political asylum in the UK, and then safe passage to Afghanistan and Pakistan for training, before returning to Russia to fight in the then raging Second Chechen War. While the Chilcot Report does not raise the issue of British protection of jihadist terrorists, the fact is that the Chechen terrorists who were safe-housed, financed, and protected by the British Crown went on to form a military backbone of Al-Qaeda, and later of the Islamic State (ISIS).

Osama Bin Laden was one of the Al-Qaeda terrorists, who maintained a residence, an office, and an extensive network of supporters and recruiters throughout Britain. Even after the September 11, 2001 attacks, these official British support operations continued, to the point that London became notorious as "Londonistan," a world center for global jihadist terrorism. At the very moment that Prime Minister Tony Blair was cunningly swearing his allegiance to Bush and Cheney for the Afghan and Iraq war efforts, he was engaging in protecting Saudi-backed jihadist terrorists.

It is a sordid tale of imperial arrogance, cynicism, murder, and mayhem on a global scale.

The centerpiece of the Anglo-Saudi partnership was the oil-for-arms barter deal known as Al-Yamamah, first negotiated in 1985 between Blair's predecessor, Margaret Thatcher, and Saudi Prince Bandar Bin Sultan, the longstanding Saudi Ambassador to the United States. Blair enthusiastically continued the Al-Yamamah deal when he succeeded the Tories, and expanded its scope.

In 2006, when evidence surfaced that the Al-Yamamah deal had created a string of offshore slush funds for conducting joint Anglo-Saudi black operations—including the funding of the Afghan *mujahideen*, later to spawn Al Qaeda—Blair shut down the probe, invoking British national security interests. By the time that Blair intervened to cover up the truth about the Al-Yamamah program, at least $100 billion had been amassed in offshore black accounts that exist to this day, and still continue to finance global terrorism.

FEMA News Photo/Michael Rieger
New York firefighters and rescue workers search for survivors at the site of the destroyed World Trade Center.

The 28-page chapter, long suppressed, opens a Pandora's Box of leads on the Saudi support for the 9/11 hijackers. It also opens a window into the "inside job." The very first conclusion of the chapter, which is titled "Findings, Discussion and Narrative Regarding Certain Sensitive National Security Matters," is that the FBI and the CIA were asleep at the switch prior to 9/11, and made no effort to probe the Saudi regime's links to Al-Qaeda. This was itself a stunning indictment, given that Al-Qaeda had already bombed two U.S. embassies in Africa and the USS Cole, a guided-missile destroyer in the harbor of Aden, Yemen—resulting altogether in more than 200 hundred deaths. Washington sources insist that there was a handful of intelligence agents who tirelessly pursued the Saudi/Al-Qaeda threat, but their work was suppressed as soon as Bush and Cheney came into office.

New Information in the 28 Pages

The 28-page chapter made no claim to be an exhaustive investigation into the Saudi role in 9/11. Indeed, the Joint Inquiry was severely limited by the narrow Congressional mandate, and the lack of time, staffing, and funding to do independent investigations. The staff principally reviewed files from the FBI and CIA, interviewed key personnel, and assembled investigative leads to be pursued by the later 9/11 Commission or by follow-on Congressional probes. The Joint Inquiry chapter stated up front:

Given the serious national security implications of this information [on Saudi sponsorship of Al-Qaeda and the 9/11 hijackers], however, the leadership of the Joint Inquiry is referring the staff's compilation of relevant information to both the FBI and the CIA for investigative

CC BY-SA 3.0/Mikhail Evstafiev

A Chechen fighter near the burned-out ruins of the Presidential Palace in Grozny, January 1995.

review and appropriate investigative and intelligence action.

Despite those limitations, the Joint Inquiry found that a large number of Saudi government officials, suspected government intelligence officers, and agents of the Saudi Royal Family were in direct contact with at least two of the hijackers from the moment they arrived in the United States in early 2000, having just attended an Al-Qaeda planning session in Kuala Lumpur, Malaysia, where the outlines of the 9/11 attack were first put together.

The chapter went far beyond the details of the Joint Inquiry's work that had already been revealed in Sen. Bob Graham's 2004 book, *Intelligence Matters.* That book identified two Saudi intelligence officers, Osama Basnan and Omar Al-Bayoumi, as contact points for the two original hijackers, Khalid Al-Mihdhar and Nawaf Al-Hazmi. Graham revealed that Prince Bandar and his wife Princess Haifa had regularly provided money to Basnan's wife, and that Al-Bayoumi had also been paid by a Saudi Defense and Aviation Ministry-linked company as a "ghost employee," during the time that he and Basnan were bankrolling and providing logistical support to the hijackers. Al-Bayoumi received $20,000 from the Saudi Ministry of Finance and worked as "an accountant" for the Saudi Ministry of Defense and Aviation.

During the first five months that the two San Diego-based hijackers were in the United States, under the sponsorship of Al-Bayoumi and Basnan, Al-Bayoumi made almost one hundred telephone calls to Saudi government officials at the Saudi Embassy in Washington, the Saudi Cultural Mission in Washington, and the Saudi Consulate in Los Angeles.

Furthermore, the 28 pages reveal that the FBI had discovered—after the 9/11 attacks—that Al-Bayoumi worked for Avco Dallah, a Saudi defense contractor with documented ties to Osama Bin Laden and Al-Qaeda. The FBI had information from an informant that Basnan boasted that he and Al-Bayoumi were in contact with the two San Diego hijackers, and that he, Basnan, "had done more" to assist the hijackers than Al-Bayoumi.

Basnan had first come to the attention of the FBI in 1993, when he hosted a party for the "blind sheikh," Omar Abdul Rahman, a key participant in the World Trade Center bombing in February of that year. At that time, Basnan had boasted to FBI informants that he was a loyal follower of Osama Bin Laden, whom he called "the official Khalifate and the ruler of the Islamic world."

Saudi Royalty, Saudi Naval Officers

The report of the Joint Inquiry also links Prince Bandar, the Saudi Ambassador, to a senior Al-Qaeda figure. The authors write,

> According to FBI documents, several of the phone numbers found in the phone book of Abu Zubaida, a senior Al-Qaeda operative captured in Pakistan in March 2002, could be linked, at least indirectly, to telephone numbers in the United States. One of those U.S. numbers is subscribed to by the ASPCOL Corporation, which is located in Aspen, Colorado, and manages the affairs of the Colorado residence of the Saudi Ambassador Bandar.[1]

The report then notes that another number in Zubai-

1. The text of the 28-page chapter is at http://intelligence.house.gov/sites/intelligence.house.gov/files/documents/declasspart4.pdf. This extract is from pages 418-419 of the report, which are the fourth and fifth pages of the text of the chapter.

da's phone book, confiscated when he was captured, was that of a security guard at the Saudi Embassy in Washington.

Prince Bandar was also suspected of financing the Islamic Assembly of North America (IANA). The 28-page chapter reports that, "according to the FBI, IANA's mission is actually to spread Islamic fundamentalism and Salafist doctrine throughout the United States and the world at large."

The very next paragraph of the chapter reveals that,

videograb from BBC Panorama show

Saudi Prince Bandar and British Prime Minister Margaret Thatcher.

FBI documents also indicate that several Saudi Naval officers were in contact with the September 11 hijackers. FBI documents state that the San Diego Field Office opened a counterterrorism investigation on an individual named Osama Nooh, a Saudi Naval officer, due to his association with Nawaf Al-Hazmi and Khalid Al-Mihdhar. In addition, Lafi Al-Harbi, another Saudi Naval officer, was in telephonic contact with flight 77 hijacker Khalid Al-Mihdhar and Nawaf Al-Hazmi on nine occasions from March 11, 2000 to March 27, 2000.

The Jacksonville FBI Field Office is conducting an investigation to determine whether Saleh Ahmed Bedaiwi, a Saudi Naval officer within its territory, was in contact with any of the hijackers.

The next ten lines of the 28-page chapter are redacted.

Immediately after the account of the Saudi Naval officers, and the redactions, the report continues,

… according to the FBI, an individual named Fahad Abdullah Saleh Bakala was close friends with September 11 hijackers Ahmed Al-Ghamdi and Hamza Al-Ghamdi. Bakala previously "worked as a pilot for the Saudi Royal family, flying Osama Bin Laden between Afghanistan and Saudi Arabia during OBL's exile." In addition, an FBI source stated after September 11 that he/she was 50% sure that Al-Mihdhar was a visitor at an apartment in McLean, Virginia that was occupied in July and August 2001 by Hamad

Alotaiba of the Saudi Embassy Military Division. FBI documents also note that September 11 hijacker Saeed Al-Ghamdi may have also visited the address.

The concluding section of the 28-page chapter deals with the failures of the FBI to act on intelligence that they had in their possession, dating back to the mid-1990s, even before the Africa embassy bombings. It is a stunning account of mass incompetence—at best.

What the missing chapter now makes clear is that, as Representatives Jones, Lynch, and Massie emphasized, the FBI top management, starting with Director Robert Mueller, remained willfully clueless about actionable intelligence in their own files against the 9/11 hijackers and their Saudi official sponsors.

What To Do

September 11 widow Kristen Breitweiser wrote in *Huffington Post*, the day after the release of the 28-page chapter, that Congress must act immediately by reconvening on an emergency basis to vote Saudi Arabia onto the list of State Sponsors of Terrorism.

The United Kingdom should be added to the same list, based on the massive evidence of the Anglo-Saudi offshore funding mechanisms, used to finance actions like 9/11.

Obama must be suspended from his functions under the 25th Amendment and placed on trial for complicity in covering up British-Saudi terrorism, and for launching wars of aggression based on lies, just as Blair, Bush, and Cheney did.

Undo the Paradigm Shift Resulting From the Assassination of Herrhausen

During a discussion period at the July 23 Northwest Strategic Seminar in Seattle, Washington, entitled: "Humanity at the Brink—The United States Must Join the Eurasian Project," Helga Zepp-LaRouche responded to a question concerning the necessity of saving Deutsche Bank, as follows:

Zepp-LaRouche: Let me just add this, because people may not be familiar with the significance of Alfred Herrhausen. Alfred Herrhausen was the chairman of Deutsche Bank at the time when the Berlin Wall came down, and he was assassinated at the end of November, actually three weeks after the Berlin Wall had come down. And that particular murder had as much significance for the paradigm shift to the worst in Germany, as the assassination of John F. Kennedy did for the United States.

If you remember, Kennedy was very, very optimistic. He had the idea of space travel, of unlimited self-perfection of human beings, of overcoming poverty in the developing countries—just an *absolute* optimistic world outlook and image of man. And when he was killed and his murder was covered up, the people of the United States became pessimistic, so much so that recently I have been saying that Americans are almost as pessimistic as the Germans.

But for Germany, this was absolutely crucial, because—maybe the older ones among you remember the unbelievable circumstances when the Wall came down and people from East Germany came, adancing on the Berlin Wall, hugging each other, crying; it was an unbelievable moment in history.

And if Herrhausen would have continued to be the advisor of Helmut Kohl, the whole question of unification would have taken a completely different turn, because he was the last moral banker, in Europe, at least that I know of. He wanted to forgive the debt of the Third World because, he said, this debt is not payable anyway. He wanted to put the European, German-Russian relationship on an even level. He wanted to develop Poland with the means of the *Kreditanstalt* used in the reconstruction of postwar Germany. So he had many, many sound policies, and all the people who knew him, said that he was a great human being, more important even than being a great banker.

His car was blown up as a message to Helmut Kohl: "Do not dare to use the moment of German unification to develop an independent, sovereign policy." And then, as we now know, Margaret Thatcher launched a campaign against Germany. Mitterrand, according to Jacques Attali who was one of his closest advisors and who wrote a biography of Mitterrand, wrote that Mitterrand threatened Germany with war at that moment, if Germany would not be ready to give up [its sovereign currency] the D-mark and replace it with the European common currency, the euro.

Kohl knew at the time that the European common currency would not work without political union, and that the euro was against German interests; but he was basically surrounded by France, Britain, and the United States who all told him, you better capitulate and give up the D-mark as the price for unification.

So it was really this murder of Alfred Herrhausen which is the reason that the great historical chance of 1989 did not lead to a new peace order of the 21st Century, which at that time would have been possible.

We then proposed—especially Lyn, the development of the Productive Triangle Paris-Berlin-Vienna. This is an area the size of Japan, and still has the most productive concentration of especially the very productive, very innovative, very creative *Mittelstand*, the middle-level industry. The idea was to take that and develop what we called "development corridors" to Poland, to Ukraine, to the Balkans, and transform the Comecon countries with Western technology. And when the Soviet Union disintegrated in '91, we expanded that Productive Triangle to become the Eurasian Land-Bridge, to provide development corridors combining the industrial and population centers of Europe with those of Asia, through transport and development corridors: And that is what we called, already then, the New Silk Road.

So we campaigned for this, for 25, 26 years, and now it is very good that the New Silk Road is on the agenda. But all the destruction of Russia from '91 to '94, whereby the industrial potential of Russia was destroyed, and collapsed to only *one-third*, was the result of the same geopolitical policies which had led to the murder of Herrhausen. And if you want to cure this policy, including the war danger, which right now is very, very acute, we have to go back and change the policies, do a reset.

And Deutsche Bank is about to blow—as a matter of fact, just yesterday, reports were leaked that they're considering giving up universal banking and instead have an internal separation of their banking branches between the commercial branch which gives credit to industry, and separating that completely from their investment branch, which is quite an admission, because Deutsche Bank was always considered *the* universal banking model and now they basically admit that this is not working.

Obviously, such reform alone is not sufficient, but it is an interesting reflection of our campaign. So I would like to encourage you to study this period of history, because the connection between the murder of Kennedy and the murder of Herrhausen, gives you the clue of where things went wrong in the history of both the United States and Germany. And if you want to remedy it, we have to get the United States back on the track of Roosevelt and Kennedy and we have to get Germany back on the track of Alfred Herrhausen, if we want to get out of this crisis.

So please do not block on this campaign.

www.ingramcontent.com/pod-product-compliance
Lightning Source LLC
Chambersburg PA
CBHW080325290526
45793CB00006B/1215